First Names in Gifting

THE STORY OF HARRY & DAVID

by GAIL SNYDER

First Names in Gifting

Editorial Director	Rob Levin
Managing Editor	Sarah E. Fedota
Harry & David Liaison	Rhonda Klug
Publisher	Barry Levin
Chief Operating Officer	Renée Peyton
Author	Gail Snyder
Design	Laurie Porter
Prepress	Jill Dible
Copyediting and Indexing	Bob Land

© 2009 Harry & David

2500 South Pacific Highway
Medford, Oregon 97501
www.harryanddavid.com

Book Development by
Bookhouse Group, Inc.
Atlanta, Georgia
www.bookhouse.net

Printed in Canada
ISBN: 978-0-615-31645-1

Dedicated seasonal
workers, circa 1930s.

Contents

Time doesn't alter the bountiful beauty of the Rogue River Valley where Harry & David's Royal Riviera® Pears have been nurtured and harvested for seventy-five years.

Foreword

Those first Harry & David customers seventy-five years ago were delighted to receive their shipment of Harry & David Royal Riviera® Pears. One can only imagine the expressions on their faces as they opened the gift to reveal their beautifully presented Harry & David treats. Inside they saw each pear carefully packed for the long trip across the country. These pears had just arrived in perfect condition all the way from Medford, Oregon! Quite a feat back in the 1930s.

The two brothers faced tremendous challenges as they launched their business, not the least of which was shipping Royal Riviera® Pears from one coast to the other. Although much has changed since 1934, and Harry & David is a far more complex enterprise than it was back then, we haven't lost sight of keeping our promises to our customers and our links to the past. We are still growing Royal Riviera® Pears on some of the very same orchard land that our founders' father farmed, and each one of our gifts is still packed with pride. Just as Harry and David believed, we know that our success begins and ends with good people— skilled, hardworking, and honest people who do everything from growing Royal Riviera® Pears and making luscious chocolates to taking customer orders, working in our stores, and shipping the gifts our customers love to give.

Today, Harry & David is an important part of the American holiday gifting tradition. Our catalogs, Web site, and stores provide gifts for millions of American families and businesses, and as you read about our seventy-five-year history, you'll discover a company with a rich heritage. Although we have changed with the times, we remain faithful to the core values that are at the foundation of the company and that serve as its guiding principles. I like to think that Harry and David are looking on approvingly at the way we've added to their legacy.

Bill Williams
President and Chief Executive Officer
Harry & David

B. B. Lowry *(left)* and David Holmes discuss the 1939 harvest. Samuel Rosenberg, Harry and David's father, hired Lowry as the foreman of Bear Creek Orchards in the early 1900s.

However, while much has changed,
much has also remained the same . . .

Once not for the fainthearted, with shorter trees pear picking has become much safer with three-quarters of the fruit accessible from the ground.

The Fruits of Their Labor
Orchards Come to the Rogue River Valley

After a long winter's rest, the fruit trees of the Rogue River Valley spring to life and the spectacular cycle of the pear orchards begins anew.

INTRODUCTION

THE FRUITS OF THEIR LABOR
ORCHARDS COME TO THE ROGUE RIVER VALLEY

*I*n a cool morning breeze, glossy green leaves ripple as the sun rolls up the distant mountain ridge on its daily climb to warm the hills of Oregon's Rogue River Valley. Workers form a loose circle in the damp grass and discuss the day's plans, seemingly accustomed to the breathtaking scene surrounding them—an orchard for as far as the eye can see, growing ripe with pears.

To the untrained eye, this orchard may appear untouched by time. The year could be 1885, when J. H. Stewart planted the first large pear orchards in the valley, proudly shipping a commercial carload of his crop within five years. It could be 1886, when Arthur Weeks (Stewart's son-in-law) and his brothers established Bear Creek Orchard, the second in the valley, naming it after the sparkling creek that ran through the land, and nursed it to success until the turn of the century. But to those who have lived for decades in this mountain-flanked region, the visual changes that have taken place in the orchards over the years are obvious and significant. Of course, some changes can be seen, but many changes can only be told, related through the personal stories of hardworking people who have survived and thrived in this valley through the fruits of their labor.

Encouraged by the success of their Royal Riviera® Pears, ▶
the brothers built the first cold storage warehouse in the
Rogue River Valley. Little did they know in this 1920s photo
that the stock market crash was right around the corner.

The harvest continues from August through October. Then the trees go into dormancy, resting peacefully before once again bearing fruit.

◄ **Ron Henri, recently retired senior** vice president of orchards, says of his long career at Harry & David: "I'm one of those generations of growers that have taken on the challenges of Comice. It's a fickle crop to grow, but we've got it down!"

"Isn't this a nice setting? It is one of the last areas in the valley that is still largely agricultural," says Ron Henri, retired senior vice president of orchards. Henri was here when this four-hundred-acre tract was purchased in 1998. He explains that this particular orchard was rebuilt from scratch and is now in the stages of yielding its fifth crop of pears.

Henri recalls how he, as a young and eager new employee, began his own pear-harvesting experience. "It was my first year. I

> *""When's a good time to pick these pears?' And he asked, 'Well, when do you want to pick them?'"*

walked up to my boss, who was then the vice president of the orchards, and asked, 'When's a good time to pick these pears?' And he asked, 'Well, when do you want to pick them?'" Henri chuckles.

The fondly remembered conversation from 1974 reflects what was then a more casual approach to the

▲ **Even through decades of change, because** of the orchards, the breathtaking vistas of the Rogue River Valley remain much the same.

The fruit of Bear Creek Orchards quickly outgrew its first home—the original packinghouse pictured here. In 1923 the company built one of the Rogue River Valley's first pear pre-cooling plants, a major innovation for the industry at that time.

Harry & David orchard business. "When I first started working here, the original family was the executive management of the company, and it was a lot more laid back," says Henri. "It was busy, but there were gaps when we could stop and talk, just visit and get caught up. It was a farming-community culture, and a hunting-and-fishing culture." (In fact, the orchard growers often begged the seasonal workers not to go into the foothills for such pursuits because the growers knew that their labor force might disappear for days during peak pear-picking time.) "That's changed," says Henri. "As always, everybody gets up in the morning and does the work they have to do to grow this crop. But it's more proce-dural now out of necessity because the business has grown exponentially."

However, while much has changed, much has also remained the same. Today Harry & David's thirty-four hundred acres of land holdings continue to benefit from a delicate microclimate combined with rich soils and drainage systems that help the fruit trees come in early;

crystal-pure snowmelt irrigation water, absent chemical alteration; and dedicated, documented workers always devoted to bringing in the highest-quality crops. Yes, many things have changed, but as Henri states, "Harvest is still harvest, wherever you go."

But this isn't just any crop. With the exception of several blocks of the Bosc variety used for pollination, these trees boast a type of pear so succulent and historically desired by aristocrats and royalty that it has been called "The Fruit of Kings"—the Doyenne du Comice pear.

The Comice pear—a fickle fruit to grow—was first developed in France in 1849. As fragile as it was delicious, the rare fruit was favored by members of the ruling class and was served in the finest European restaurants. A winter pear, the Comice demanded a delicate climate and soil combination found in few regions of the world. One of those places turned out to be Medford, Oregon.

Introduced to Oregon's Rogue River Valley in 1897, trees of the Comice variety were eventually grafted to the roots of the sturdier Winter Nelis pear tree and "the prince of pears" began to take to the valley that would soon be heir to a "royal" future. A passage from *Sunset* magazine describes the foreign fruit's debut to a larger audience, a premiere that would eventually prove to be the saving grace of the regional pear industry:

> Its size is usually large, the pear often weighing as much as a pound. But its taste, its regal quality! . . . A slight flavor of the pineapple, sucre, and the faintest suggestion of the most delicate, the most

The difficulty and dangers of harvest were minimized in the 1960s when the roots of the Comice were grafted to quince root, which dwarfed tree height but didn't compromise fruit quality.

exquisite blend of something Oriental that tropical climes alone can produce. What that indescribable something is, makes the Doyenne du Comice world-famed.

But this was a different world—America—where every man and woman held their fate in their own hands and made daily decisions that could result in failure, fortune, or sometimes both. Many of the people who worked the lands of southern Oregon and tried their hands as orchardists had come and gone, discouraged by the bone-grinding labor, the catastrophes that weather could suddenly bring, and the endless battles with bugs and beasts that consumed their potential harvests. However, others stayed. They persisted. In 1975, the *Medford Mail Tribune* well described the demands of the fruit industry that has now operated for over a century in the Rogue River Valley: "It requires a particular and uncommon type of individual to manage it—part farmer, part businessman, part labor-negotiator, part gambler, part scientist and all rugged individualist."

Such were the individuals who stoically endured blight, drought, hailstorms, and damaging winds to sustain their livelihoods. Together they grew the state's fruit industry and prepared the way for people such as Samuel Rosenberg, who in turn developed the land and the orchards for his sons, Harry and David. The rest is history, a history that merges with the strong promise of an ongoing successful future.

▼ **The machine hasn't yet been invented** that can harvest pears without damaging the delicate fruit. A practiced picker fills a bin per hour, which holds approximately four hundred pounds of pears.

The *Pear* Pioneers

The Weeks and Orr Orchard, 1895, covered many acres and was one of the few operations that survived through the hard times of the twentieth century.

Arthur Weeks, Bear Creek Orchard's originator, may have been one of those who tired of the required toil and changing fortunes of the fruit industry. He and his brothers sold their property in 1900 to Hunt Lewis. Within several years Lewis set a world record for crop yield and for the auction price of $4,622.80 for a carload of Comice pears in New York City. Nevertheless, when a real estate syndicate named Whistler, Olwell, Clark, and Meyer approached him with an attractive offer for his orchard, Lewis sold. The real estate firm, in turn, placed the orchard on the market.

Possibly impressed by an exhibit of the orchard's pears at the 1909 Alaska-Yukon-Pacific Exposition, where Bear Creek Orchard's Comice and d'Anjou pears won several first prizes, a Seattle businessman by the name of Samuel Rosenberg inquired about the property. In 1910, Rosenberg, previously a clothier, Alaskan gold-mining outfitter, and owner of the luxury Hotel Sorrento in Seattle, Washington, purchased these 237 prime acres of fruit trees in the Rogue River Valley for $300,000.

At that time, he may appropriately have been viewed as a greenhorn by those who had committed generations to the backbreaking and often frustrating labor that is the lot of a professional orchardist. Much of the physically demanding work was simply dealing with the animals. David Lowry, whose father Bert was the orchard's first foreman, remembers hearing his

As delectable as the Comice pears appear, they are seldom taken from the orchards, because uninformed thieves soon learn that this fruit requires specific postharvest conditioning before attaining peak tasty perfection.

After building the first state-of-the-art cold storage building in the early 1920s, Harry & David continued to perfect the fruit cooling technique. Currently they use approximately 287,900 square feet of cold storage. An additional 360,000 square feet capacity of extra cold storage is rented for peak requirements.

father discuss those early days: "The spray rigs, all the wagons, everything was horse and mule power. About half the effort and energy in the fruit industry was devoted to feeding and caring for these animals. There were huge barns on all the orchards."

Yet, with a love of agriculture driving him on and a sense of humor to support his determination, Rosenberg joked that by trading a less-than-profitable hotel for this venture he had literally "traded a lemon for a pear." (Though he often said that he had traded the Hotel Sorrento for the land, the rumor was never verified, but possibly kept alive by Rosenberg's quip.) Rosenberg surely couldn't have imagined that Bear Creek Orchards would make him the founding father of one of the most successful companies in the history of the state.

At first, Samuel's two sons—Harry and David—were not quite as enamored of the pear orchard business as their father. Though they had both earned degrees in agriculture at New York's Cornell University, they had plans of their own—farming and raising prize-winning merino sheep. But in 1914, at age fifty-six, Samuel Rosenberg caught pneumonia and died. The Rosenberg brothers' plans for sheep farming were put on hold as their career path took a detour—and the road led straight to a pear orchard, just south of Medford, Oregon.

Within several years, long-sought-after irrigation systems and land availability beckoned people to the valley and pumped new life into the fruit industry. Better access to water quenched many of the anxieties associated with sustaining orchards, and the fruit-laden valley just south

▲ **These 1939 pear harvesters were largely migrant workers** who enjoyed the picking season at Bear Creek, where they received a fair wage, room and board, and three square meals daily.

of the newly paved and prosperous streets of Medford became known as "Little Italy." Harry and David constructed a new packing shed and built a cold storage unit for their crops along the Southern Pacific railroad tracks. Their first cold storage plant—fifty by eighty feet, two stories high, with thirteen-foot ceilings—held twenty cars of fruit per floor and was filled to capacity three times per season. In 1924, theirs was the only cold storage plant in the valley owned by a single firm, and the pre-cooling of their pear crop extended the fruits' freshness for sales in European markets and America's eastern states to six weeks as opposed to one or two.

The fruit crops, including the famous Comice pear, proved bountiful in the fall of 1929, but by October the bottom fell out of America's stock

Pick a Pail of Pears

Marketing magic and showmanship were two of Harry and David's talents, but they were also innovators. The two designed a pail that enabled workers to harvest with both hands, increasing productivity by 10 to 25 percent. In 1925, the *Jackson County News* applauded the brothers, noting that a local sheet metal company kept twelve local men busy fabricating one hundred pails a day for the orchard.

Even today, pickers deposit picked pears in a bucket harnessed from their shoulders. "Can five hundred pickers pick more today than they could years ago because of different tools and machinery?" mulls Ron Henri, Harry & David's retired senior vice president of orchards. "It's interesting. We've tried picking machines and other aids, but they damage the fruit. We just haven't seen a lot of advances in terms of harvesting machinery, so all pears still have to be picked very carefully by hand."

▲ **A modern version of the picking pail patented by Harry & David in 1925 leaves both** hands free for harvesting and reduces bruising of the fruit.

market. The fruit industry, like many American industries, was hard hit. The story of one orchardist who sold his land and equipment after many years of hardship and invested all of the proceeds in stocks just months prior to the crash symbolized the type of sorrow and despair experienced throughout the region. As the people of Medford suffered through the Great Depression, feelings of neighborliness seemed to wane, too. Local political battles, business disagreements, and festering animosities went hand-in-hand with job and property loss. Little did the city's citizens realize that their economy wouldn't recover until the onset of World War II.

The Great Depression drastically changed the harvest process as well. For many years, Jackson County's residents had typically pitched in each season to pick the valley's fruit, but now they were joined by an increasing number of migrant workers, thousands of them, roaming from place to place looking for work and returning for harvest every year, temporarily earning a steady wage plus good food and housing at the orchard bunkhouses during their stay.

But Harry and David weren't willing to give up yet. They struggled as 1930 and 1931 brought them closer and closer to quitting the business they had worked to build. With resorts and restaurants of their Pacific Northwest customers shutting down, coupled with a worldwide depression, the brothers found themselves in a precarious position. Many of the trees they had nurtured since the turn of the century were now in their prime and hanging heavy with beautiful pears. They journeyed to their father's old stomping grounds, Seattle, and peddled samples of their pears to local businessmen, asking them, "Wouldn't you like to give fruit as delicious as this to your clients, suppliers, or family members?" Promising to deliver a gift box of prime,

The original Comice pear orchards in the Rogue River Valley were planted in standard-size trees reaching over twenty-five feet high. In later years, the orchards were replanted with shorter, more easily harvested trees.

The pear has to be picked at the stem, so that the hand doesn't break the flesh of the fruit.

A Promising Pear

At first, American buyers weren't completely sold on Harry and David's Comice crop. Sure the pears were delicious, but buyers were interested in volume. They wanted to pack as many pears as possible in a crate and sell them for five cents each, but the large, delectable Comice weighed as much as a pound each. This didn't pose a big problem for the brothers. Cosmopolitan citizens in cities such as London, Paris, and Havana craved the Comice as an elegant dessert, and the valley's pear market typically pulled in $5 million per year. Maybe Harry and David hadn't yet cornered all of the markets, but they had cornered a brand. As a foreshadowing of their future promotional prowess, they named their Oregon-grown Comice the Royal Riviera® Pear, a name that increased in fame throughout the Roaring Twenties.

sweet, ripe pears to anyone in the United States for $1.95 express paid, they succeeded in procuring quite a few orders. Encouraged, they tried the same approach in San Francisco and received more orders. Within a year, repeat orders arrived from their customers and their customers' friends and relatives. Something clicked in the minds of these young entrepreneurs.

Harry and David were no longer selling fruit. They were selling a gift.

The two began compiling a mailing list and in 1934 sent their first mailing—the predecessor to Harry & David's most prominent and promising marketing strategy for years to come. They had hit upon a dynamic new concept. Harry and David were no longer selling fruit. They were selling a gift. The time was ripe to pack some pears and leave town. Destination—New York City.

Workers spend a lot of time padding the bins before loading them with fruit. Airtight trailers are later used for transport.

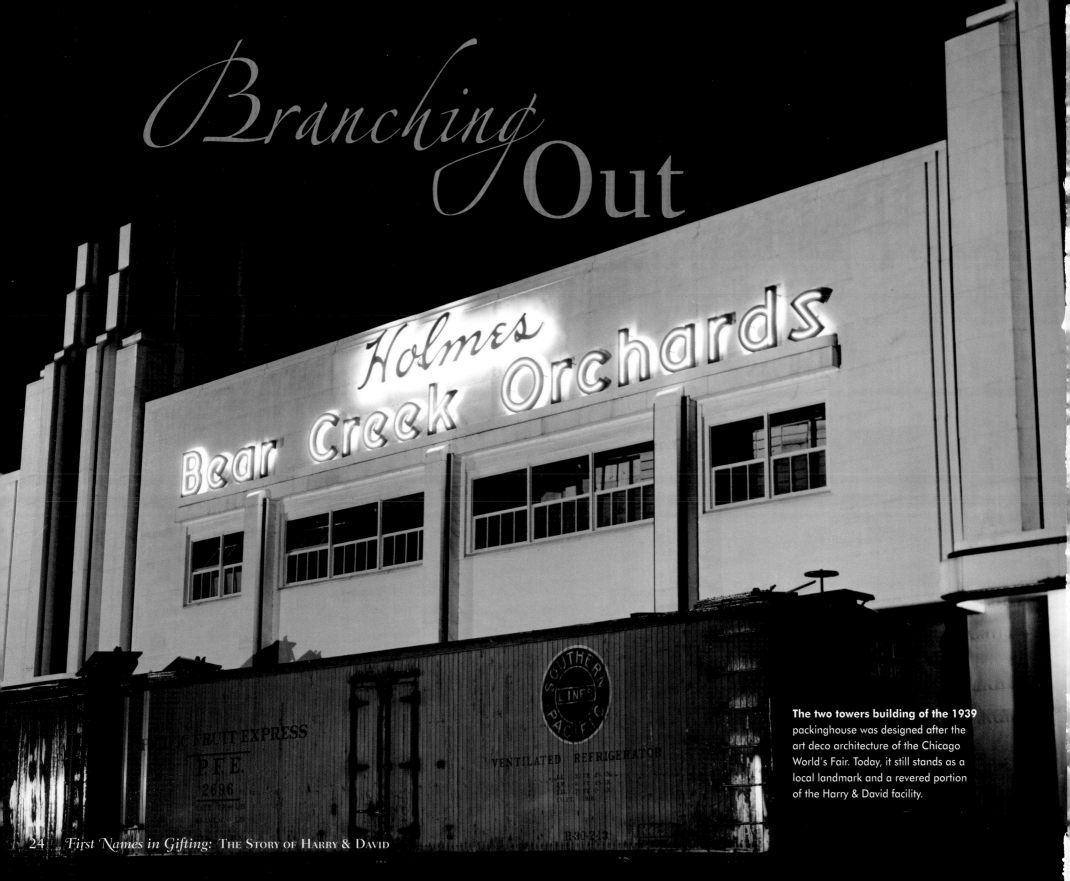

Branching Out

The two towers building of the 1939 packinghouse was designed after the art deco architecture of the Chicago World's Fair. Today, it still stands as a local landmark and a revered portion of the Harry & David facility.

CHAPTER 2

BRANCHING OUT

Alone in New York City with fifteen boxes of Royal Riviera® Pears to keep him company, Harry Rosenberg couldn't gain access to the movers and shakers of the Big Apple, as he had hoped. One evening, he related his plight to an empathetic listener at a party. The stranger suggested he call G. Lynn Sumner, a remarkable advertising agent with contacts that included the cream of the crop of New York's business elite. The next day, Harry did just that, phoning from his room at the Waldorf Astoria Hotel. "You don't know me and I don't know you," Harry began the phone call, "but last evening a man whose name I didn't get suggested that I call." Intrigued, Sumner and several associates paid Harry and his pears a visit.

Harry told Sumner that he had been in the city for a week and had made no progress in his efforts to introduce the city's executives to his rapidly ripening pears. Sumner recalled later that Harry "had brought along from Oregon fifteen boxes of Comice pears and they were ripening on him quickly. He had been living with the pears in that room for a week, and they had just about forty-eight hours to go."

After the meeting with Harry, Sumner and his team grabbed as many sheets of Waldorf-Astoria stationery as they could get their hands on and penned a letter from the perspective of the two brothers,

David Holmes (1939) proudly lets the ▶
succulent Royal Riviera® Pear take
center stage.

speaking as simple folks from out west. The next day, fifteen prominent business executives—including Walter Chrysler, David Sarnoff (head of RCA and later NBC), and Owen Young (chairman of General Electric)—received the hand-delivered letters, each message closely followed by the delivery of a box of Royal Riviera® Pears. The letter urged these decision makers to sample the fruit and to then consider the pleasure that a gift of such pears (at only $1.95 a box with shipping and sent straight from the orchards) would bring to friends and family. Within the hour Walter Chrysler summoned Harry to his office, where Chrysler placed an order for gift-boxed pears. Within twenty-four hours, eleven of the fifteen recipients had ordered a total of 489 boxes of the incomparable Royal Riviera® Pears.

▲ Harry & David's customers always expect the very best, and the company's fruit basket assemblers and inspectors have always made sure that gift recipients aren't just satisfied—they're delighted.

These 1939 pear graders let only the perfect pears pass as gift fruit. The remainder, just as tasty, were diverted for commercial packing.

▲ **Harry & David representatives traveled the world in search of mysterious and exotic offerings** for the Fruit-of-the-Month Club®, including New Zealand kiwi berries and Chinese gooseberries.

One can only imagine the elation Harry must have felt on his return to Oregon with almost five hundred orders from the movers and shakers of American business. With an innate sense of timing and savvy for promotion, Harry and David composed a four-page flyer singing the praises of their pears. Before 1934 was over, they had sold an unprecedented six thousand gift boxes. By the following year, business had more than doubled, with shipments surpassing fifteen thousand boxes. The first direct-mail business for gift fruit had blossomed.

Next it was David's turn to visit New York City and meet with G. Lynn Sumner—the man responsible for seeding the quality reputation of Harry and David's pears. David was open to Sumner's suggestion of a national advertising campaign, although taken aback when Sumner suggested that the opening salvo

Once the concept was created, Harry and David never stopped developing new ideas for the Fruit-of-the-Month Club® gift, and the brothers' successors diligently honor that tradition today. First offered as a three-box club containing pears, apples (Golden Delicious renamed Golden Bears), and Oregold® peaches (also a brand name created by Harry and David), the club quickly extended to a twelve-month series. Alphonse Lavelle grapes, Royal oranges, grapefruit, fresh Hawaiian pineapples, exotic nectarines, and kiwi berries arrived in perfect condition with money-back satisfaction guaranteed.

Then as today, each perfect shipment was picked, planned, and packed with the goal of thrilling the customer. As one of those responsible for the worldwide outsourcing of fruit, John Roberts, former senior vice president of fruit acquisition for Harry & David until his retirement in 2008, traveled the globe in search of fruit that could pass the company's rigid quality tests. "The Southern Hemisphere is one of our favorite haunts because their seasons are just the opposite of ours," he explains, although some of their suppliers were not so far-flung. "When I was with the company, part of every manager's duty was to spend time each year at an outside location, packing whatever item was in the Fruit-of-the-Month Club® gift. I spent many a day packing nectarines, plums, and oranges in California and grapefruit in Florida and Texas."

When a shipping strike once delayed orders of Hawaiian pineapples, the brothers had them flown by plane to avoid disappointing customers. This same attention to customer service continues today, not only with the Fruit-of-the-Month Club® gift, but with every product—so much so that the holiday wish lists of employees as well as long-term customers always include Harry & David gifts. "When I buy Christmas gifts for my family or friends, I buy them the Fruit-of-the-Month Club® gift because it's something I know they will use, that I know they will appreciate, and it's the best quality they can get," says Nancy Tait, retired Harry & David president.

◀ **The Fruit-of-the-Month Club®, launched in 1936, greatly expanded** sales throughout the year. Harry (*left*) and David look over one of the gifts under a banner that also features Cubby Bear (1948).

▲ **Harry and David demonstrate that the pears are as plump as ever in this** 1948 photo taken after the company not only survived but thrived throughout the Great Depression and World War II.

A Friendly Fortune

"Out here on the ranch, we don't know much about advertising, and maybe we're foolish to spend the price of a tractor on this space, but . . . we believe you folks who read *Fortune* are the kind of folks who'd like to know our story."

These were the homespun words that introduced Harry and David to the world in an ad so effective that it not only became the trademark tone for the brothers' continuing campaign but won the advertising industry's best magazine advertisement of the year in 1937. In 1949, the ad was also recognized in Watkins's *One Hundred Greatest Advertisements*. Retaining the "just folks" approach in future communications resulted in customers who felt just like family, as one of thousands of customer letters attests: "It's sort of like ordering from your aunt or uncle, and you know they will do their durndest because they love you."

▲ Our motto, "So big and juicy, you eat them with a spoon.®"

This early Harry & David display in Penn Station, New York, predicted the future of the brothers' flair for public relations and public promotion.

should be a full-page ad in *Fortune* magazine. After pausing a moment to take it all in, David said aloud to himself, "Imagine Harry and me advertising our pears in *Fortune*." Those became the first words for an ad that crafted the down-home flavor and, at times, cornpone image that Sumner created for the two brothers.

Though far from fitting the profile of two hayseeds, Harry and David didn't mind such stereotypes in their advertisements; in fact, the brothers participated in perpetuating them. They adopted a we're-just-like-you familiarity that brought customers closer with ads that read like letters to family members . . . a family larger by the day due to a growing staff and an expanding customer base, now that their market was no longer limited to European aris-

> ## "Imagine Harry and me advertising our pears in Fortune."

tocracy or the American elite. Harry and David reached out to every man, woman, and child who yearned for the luscious experience of eating a juicy dessert pear with a spoon. With personable ads in such well-known publications as *National Geographic, Time,* and *The New York Times,* the brothers matched their pears with an affordable price and enticed the populace with the question, "Aren't there people right here in America who would appreciate such rare delicacies just as much as royalty?" Apparently many Americans thought so.

Despite a flourishing business, by 1937 Harry and David faced another dilemma. The Royal Riviera® Pear, a winter pear harvested in early fall, made the perfect product for the

▲ **Why use a ladder when an elephant is available?**
David Holmes, in another of his playful publicity pranks, picks pears with a pachyderm.

Imagine Harry and Me advertising our PEARS in Fortune!

· 155 ·

holidays when so many fruits were out of season. But after the holidays, the business of the day was hurry up and wait. Wait for the winter to end, wait for the pear trees to blossom, wait for harvest, and wait for the next bustling season.

Harry, a brilliant businessman with a conservative bent, and David, a prankster with a creative flair, formed the perfect synergistic team. Together they often came up with new, on-target products and marketing schemes that appealed to a diversity of tastes and taste buds. How, they wondered, would customers like to receive or send a box of fruit each month?

Originally called the "Box of the Month" and then renamed the "Rare Fruit Club," today the Fruit-of-the-Month Club® gift is one of the company's most popular products. In 1938, the company took in an astonishing eighty-seven thousand orders with this program. The daunting task had become filling the orders pouring in from around the country.

A broadened product line meant expanding the boundaries of fruit acquisition outside of Oregon territory. Harry and David soon began their exploration of America, and eventually the world, seeking the most unusual, highly desirable, and finest fruits available. Their search was driven by one unalterable requirement—the same foremost requirement ingrained in the company's culture today: quality.

▲ **The Rare Fruit Club, described in this** 1937 brochure, introduced America to unusual fruits from around the globe.

Building a Future

Though the Rosenbergs adhered to a plan of conservative growth, they had outgrown their place of business. Throughout the years, they had added storing sheds and lean-tos to their original plant, but a growing business demanded expanded facilities. In 1937, a new unit expanded packing capability to three hundred boxes an hour, the equivalent of fifteen freight cars every nine hours. "Our present plant, we hope, will represent the modern pear packing plant in the West," said David. "We feel that our new plant is designed in every detail to handle those perishable fruit as nearly perfectly as the very latest developments permit." The new packing plant included yet another idea developed and patented four years earlier by the Rosenbergs and Burton B. Lowry—the circular table method of packing.

Designed by renowned architect Frank Clark to emulate the art deco designs of the 1934 Chicago World's Fair, the 1937 building featured two towers encased in stainless steel, a monument to modernism facing east on South Pacific Highway. Today, after a massive renovation in 1985, the structure still stands as part of Harry & David's headquarters, and though its towers are no longer accessible for viewing the surrounding countryside, the building remains as a symbolic sentinel of quality and a treasured Rogue Valley landmark.

An Entrepreneurial Pear

David Holmes *(left)* and his right-hand man B. B. Lowry, the steadfast and capable foreman of the orchards, forged a lifetime friendship based on common goals of quality (1939).

CHAPTER 3

AN ENTREPRENEURIAL PEAR

*I*n 1938, when many orchards had since been tilled under for farmland and commercial orchardists struggled or changed trades, Harry and David's mail-order business turned golden in the Oregon sun. Despite the shadow of the Great Depression still lingering behind them, it was a prosperous and invigorating year for the two brothers, and they purchased Ross Lane Orchard, Hollywood Orchard (then the largest Comice pear orchard in the world), and others. By year's end, they had doubled their land holdings, constructed a state-of-the-art packing plant, added cold storage capabilities, and continued to grow their Fruit-of-the-Month Club® gift and seasonal gift business. In the same year, Bear Creek Orchards set a record pear price with an order of two Christmas gift packages containing twenty-four Royal Riviera® Pears each, made even pricier by the destination and method—to Manila by Clipper plane. With shipping charges included, this order brought in a then whopping $1.77 per pear!

Yet as Harry and David's business marched ahead, the first steps toward war resounded around the world, coupled with a growing global anti-Semitism. Reading the signs of the times, Harry and David made a personal decision. Following a visit by their mother and their stepfather John (Jack) R. Holmes, a businessman who had always taken a keen interest in the orchards, they adopted his surname.

David Holmes told his foreman's son, David Lowry, "I can't wait to wake up in the morning and come down to the office and plan all these exciting things."

No one can say if this name change made a difference in Bear Creek's business opportunities at home or abroad, but the stars continued to shine on Harry and David. Despite the shortages and sacrifice that World War II brought for many, orders continued to pour in at a steady rate. "Most successes are a combination of things, including having a reasonable amount of intelligence and a sufficient amount of capital. They had both," said David Lowry, their foreman's son. "During World War II, there was a tremendous scarcity of economic goods, and they arrived on the scene with gift packages when there was nothing else to give." Only occasionally were Harry and David unable to fill an order. When that occurred, customers were quickly reimbursed and simultaneously amused with often comical apology letters containing such lines as "We feel lower than a flat-footed gopher."

At one point during the war, the brothers worried because of a serious lack of manpower. Because of the number of men serving overseas and women working in the munitions plants, not enough workers were available for harvest. David, as always, had a plan. He united the pear growers in the valley and, with the help of Senator Charles L. McNary and other politicians, asked Congress for a favor: could the soldiers at nearby Camp White and those stationed in nearby agricultural

▲ **Delivering rapidly ripening fresh fruit to recipients around the country**
via rail and road during the late 1930s could prove tricky. "No doubt about it, they did a lot of magical things back then," says Don Cato, senior vice president and general manager of customer operations.

SOMETIMES OUR FRUIT IS JUST TOO TEMPTING . . .
and though we never seek bad news, we certainly do welcome such a friendly letter as yours when a shipment is not received intact and in perfect condition.

Your thoughtfulness gives us the privilege and pleasure of making an adjustment to please you.

Your report provides an opportunity to improve our service and, as well, to insist that the Express Agency be more careful in handling our perishable shipments.

Thank you.

Harry and David

▲ **Ensuring top quality remains a key factor in Harry & David's** ongoing success. The company guaranteed satisfaction from its beginnings as evidenced by this 1945 customer postcard.

◀ **A pair of girls pose with pears** from the 1939 harvest shortly after Bear Creek Orchards set a new price record for the Rogue River Valley fruit—two boxes shipped to Manila at $1.77 per pear!

A Bear of a Scapegoat

A little mascot bear named Cubby made his first appearance on the 1937 Rare Fruit Club circular and soon became a regular of Christmas mailings and Fruit-of-the-Month Club® and holiday catalogs. At the height of his fame, Cubby was honored with signature products such as a plush toy in his likeness, and the Cubby Candy Box filled with small toys and treats. Sometimes Cubby paid the price for his fame when Harry and David blamed him for lost or damaged orders and apologized for his misdeeds, but Cubby, keeping it in stride, remained cheerful as his image was gradually replaced with depictions of Harry and David. Cubby made a final appearance before his retirement in 1972 on a Fruit-of-the-Month Club® gift promotion. Now, Cubby enjoys hibernating with his family during Harry & David's busy winter season.

▲ Mischievous Cubby Bear, Harry & David's mascot, sure got around; his image even showed up on the harvesting buckets.

◀ **During the heydays of bow-tying, workers** such as these, pictured here in 1948 putting the final touch on the Tower of Treats® gift, meticulously tied up to three hundred bows per day.

▼ **An employee at the sorting bins examines** some mighty fine fruit with the Holmes brothers.

areas spend their days off picking fruit and earning some extra cash? Congress said yes, and so did many servicemen who willingly joined in the harvest.

As the war ended, so ended a restriction on building expansion.

> *Yet another new packinghouse, office, and cold storage were built to handle soaring sales.*

Yet another new packinghouse, office, and cold storage were built to handle soaring sales. (Between the years of 1945 and 1965, the company's building space quadrupled.) IBM's newest data processing technology at the time—punch cards—were a justified investment for making sense of the burgeoning tasks of filling orders, maintaining mailing lists, and completing payroll. Bear Creek Orchards was the first

▲ **The No. 1 Gift Box of Royal Riviera® Pears,** featured here in the company's 1947 Christmas Book, retains its popularity today as The Favorite® Pears.

business in the valley to implement such a system. By 1945, the Harry & David name was so well-known, surpassing the recognition factor of Bear Creek Orchards, that the brothers officially incorporated under the name of Harry and David.

Customers seldom see nor are they concerned about the daily effort that oils the wheels of the enterprise. They were more interested in the colorful catalogs chocked cover-to-cover with a seemingly endless array of goodies: fruit cakes, Bosc pears, preserves, candy-filled ceramic Santas, miniature Christmas trees, and yet another tall order of innovation: the Tower of Treats® gift. These three, four, or five tempting packages stacked one upon another, stuffed with a variety of edibles and tied with a bow, are as alluring today as they were decades ago when the brothers' vision for a new product first became a reality.

▲ **In 1934 Harry & David published the first** company catalog for mail-order sales. This pretty model graced the cover of the 1948 edition.

◀ **Continuing the tradition of seasonal** greetings to customers, this 1955 Christmas card features Santa perusing Harry & David's catalog for great gift ideas.

A-Tisket, A-Tasket

"Before my time, they used to actually weave baskets here," says Tom Forsythe, senior vice president of production, as he explains the gift basket assembly process during a tour. (It was 1938 when Harry and David first decided to produce the company's baskets.) He arrived at Harry & David in 2000. Today, producing the handmade baskets onsite is no longer economically viable, but for decades each basket that arrived on a customer's doorstep was hand-woven by talented and dexterous women, some who spent their entire careers artfully creating the fanciful containers.

Seeking control of quality and standardization, the company originally imported rattan reed from Hong Kong for the baskets. When material supplies were interrupted during World War II, they substituted a strengthened paper that worked well due to its uniformity. Reportedly, Sybil Dodge, a bridge partner of David and his wife, designed the first basket, and Edyth Goodman was later hired to train basket weavers in a craft that was rapidly disappearing in most parts of the world.

Top weavers at the company produced up to 125 baskets per day, with fifteen weavers producing as many as 70,000 baskets during a five-month season. Skilled artisans completed a basket within ten to twelve minutes, but after a point even that rate was not enough to keep up with demands.

▲ **Even though gift baskets are created to be pleasing to the eye,** before prototypes are approved as products they are shaken, rattled, and rolled to ensure structural integrity during shipping.

In 1938 Harry & David began having baskets hand-woven ▶ onsite, but years later the volume of work made that endeavor economically unviable. However, the quality of gift baskets and the attention to detail haven't changed. The baskets are woven and filled by hand even today.

▲ **Not only do customers enjoy consuming** a delicious assortment of delicacies; they also keep a beautiful basket hand-picked by Harry & David designers.

Today, quality baskets are selected from a number of worldwide venues with two purposes in mind—to serve as protection for the fruit during shipment and as a practical keepsake thereafter. "We were able to start integrating into the line more contemporary, decorative baskets that people collect and use today. We can continually change them and update them, so people who like to receive gift baskets every year have a nice variety for different uses in their home after the fruit basket is consumed," says Nancy Tait, retired president.

These 1947 "Tower Line" employees assemble yet another of David Holmes's hit products, the Tower of Treats® gift—five packages filled with an assortment of delicacies and tied with a bow.

Harry & David started an onsite custom weaving operation in 1938. The top weavers completed as many as 125 baskets per day.

Times were good and destined to be even better. Responding to rising delivery costs, the company had developed a distribution system that sent cold storage trucks and boxcars loaded with product to thirty-nine key U.S. cities. The products were then shipped directly from their arrival point to customers throughout the cities via parcel post delivery. The Holmes brothers—"sticklers on quality," as one retiree stated—found the ultimate stickler to ensure that every bow was tied precisely, not a fingerprint resided on a jelly jar, and not a label was placed askew. His name was Glenn Harrison, an arbiter of customer service and quality control, and a man destined to become an executive vice president, as well as a legend and an example to those who worked with him in the years to come.

> *Every bow was tied precisely, not a fingerprint resided on a jelly jar, and not a label was placed askew.*

One March evening, David Holmes and office manager Nathaniel "Nat" Bender were driving down a road in San Francisco, no doubt enjoying the prospect of an upcoming spring and the blossoming of new fruit. David was at the wheel when he hit a slick spot in the road. Bender survived the accident, but David, sixty years old, succumbed to his severe injuries that evening in California's Woodland Hospital. The year was 1950. Three years later, a weakened heart forced Harry into retirement. Harry passed away in 1959 at the age of sixty-eight.

▲ **David Holmes talks with a line worker** who wraps the carefully sorted pears in Harry & David's signature gift paper (1939).

FOR PIONEERING
IN AIR SHIPPING

This certificate is presented to

Harry Holmes

in appreciation of your valuable contribution to the success of the first planeload shipment of perishables flown coast-to-coast August 23-24, 1944.

We feel confident that this historic venture marked only the beginning of what will become an important phase of future air transportation.

M.A. Patterson PRESIDENT

UNITED AIR LINES, Inc.

▲ **As innovators and dreamers the Holmes brothers were the first to fly with a new idea.** Both Harry and David received this Pioneering honor from the president of United Air Lines in 1944 for shipping the first planeload of perishables from coast to coast. With product promotion always in mind, the brothers gave a foil-wrapped pear to every United Airlines passenger who passed through Medford, Oregon.

A Man of Quality

"Glenn Harrison was so strong in the minds of those of us who worked with him for so many years because he drove the quality culture. He was the front person on quality," says John Roberts, retired senior vice president of fruit acquisition. Roberts considered Harrison his mentor, and many other Harry & David associates have a story to tell about the man who cemented the idea of "quality first" in their minds and actions. In fact, Harrison was known to collect discarded office keys and add them to the wet concrete of new building foundations to ensure they wouldn't fall into the wrong hands. He insisted that all of the screw slots in new construction were vertical to prevent them from collecting dust. Such extremes may seem eccentric, but he always had a reason for asking for perfection in every product and service. "He was a tough one, but he was a good guy," explains Roberts. "He always told us that in a production environment, if you had to make a choice between quantity and quality, always choose quality."

Janiece Newell, retired as manager of legal services after forty-one years with the company, worked with Harrison for more than sixteen years. She recalls, "He would go out on the production line and make sure that those pears were oriented in the boxes a certain way, because that was the way it was taught and that was what was expected. Most companies do not have the attention to detail in the packaging that Harry & David has maintained. He was very fair minded, but he was all about quality in product."

"He had a wonderful set of taste buds and was trained by the family, who saw that everything was sampled," remembers Perry Higgins, vice president of quality control. "I'm sure he was part of the development of our proprietary chocolate blend, and we've stuck with it." One of the original employees hired by Harry and David Holmes, Harrison died shortly after his retirement in 1985. He is remembered with fondness by many and always as a man of quality.

▲ **Glenn Harrison**

A great idea that just keeps getting better, the Tower of Treats gift, created by David Holmes, continues to be a customer favorite with too many savory options to count.

A neighbor once described Harry and David as "a couple of smart country fellows who put glamour into farming, and life into the pear deal, which was just about washed up here." It might have been an epitaph that the brothers would enjoy, but David Lowry also remembered them with great feeling: "David was tremendously personable. You wouldn't believe the number of people that went to his funeral. He was suave and outgoing. He used to say to me, 'You know, Dave, I can't wait to wake up in the morning and come down to the office and plan all these exciting things.' They were very good to me. David was very intelligent and debonair. Harry was quiet, and they were kind, thoughtful, and considerate. I admired them."

Down-home charm and juicy details ▶
were mainstays of the many newsletters sent to entice Harry & David customers—a tradition that began with the brothers' 1936 award-winning advertorial in *Fortune* magazine.

◀ **"My Brother Harry played hookey last week,"** tattled David in this 1946 folksy letter to customers that also included a photo of Harry and his big catch.

◀ **Both of the Holmes brothers were talented** businessmen, but David was the prankster, and often, the idea man for marketing and new products.

"They were very good to me. David was very intelligent and debonair. Harry was quiet, and they were kind, thoughtful, and considerate. I admired them."

Rooted in Quality

The two towers of the original Harry & David building, though now inaccessible, once provided a panoramic view of the surrounding orchards. The structure was recently updated with the new Harry & David logo.

▲ **John Holmes, son of founder Harry Holmes, ran the company capably for** nearly twenty years before selling to R. J. Reynolds Development Corp. in 1984.

◀ **David Holmes Jr, son of** founder David Holmes, created subsidiaries and made acquisitions while remaining true to the company's core business.

In a generational repeat of events, David's son, David H. Holmes, and Harry's son, John R. H. Holmes, both young men, were suddenly required, though not fully prepared, to make a multitude of decisions because of the deaths of their own fathers. A $5 million business cannot survive for long without a leader, so David—who possessed the same entrepreneurial spirit as his father—accepted the challenge. David moved the sales and marketing office to Newport Beach, California, and created several subsidiary companies, selling jewelry, toys, clothing, even a unique travel trailer, the Holiday House, a streamlined structure too ahead of its time to be economically viable for mass construction. All the while, the mail-order fruit business continued to serve as Harry & David's bread and butter.

David's efforts were not capricious. He realized that even with products such as the Fruit-of-the-Month Club® gift, the fruit packing facilities were far from fully utilized after the holidays. He wanted to provide continued work for his valued employees with year-round business earnings that would make that possible and boost the organization's profits. Called "the boldest acquisition of the company's history" up to that time, Harry & David acquired Jackson & Perkins in 1966, the largest

HOLIDAY HOUSE

CAN CHANGE YOUR WHOLE LIFE... INTERESTED?

REVOLUTION IN TRANSPORTATION: The reinforced plastics travel trailer

FEBRUARY 1961

▲ **The 1960 Geographic Model X trailer,** built by Harry and David, was twenty-four feet long and believed to be the first fiberglass trailer ever built. It featured teak walls and cabinets, a stainless steel kitchen, and a full bathroom.

▲ **David Holmes tried several new enterprises, including production of** the streamlined Holiday House. Though ahead of its time, the materials and shipping costs proved too high. "They were really nice trailers though, especially the fiberglass ones," Marshall Sellers, retired director of fruit processing, recalls.

wholesale rose producer in America. From packing smooth, cool fruit, Harry & David's employees were now also in the business of sorting and packing thorny rosebushes, but the acquisition was less than painful. The company sold exquisite rose plants not only throughout the United States, but also licensed patented roses in Japan, Korea, Mexico, South Africa, New Zealand, and Canada. Harry & David successfully owned and operated the company for over forty years before its sale in 2007.

As a spokesperson for Harry & David's Jackson & Perkins rose division, ▶ Bill Ihle, executive vice president of corporate relations, appeared not only on productions such as QVC, but sat with England's royalty, the pope, and Vatican representatives while developing commemorative rose brands.

▲ **Charles H. Perkins,** an attorney, founded the Jackson & Perkins Company with his father-in-law, Albert E. Jackson, in 1872.

After nine years, David handed the reins to his cousin John. Like his father Harry, John had a good head for business management and operations. John listened to his staff and then made the necessary moves to bring the company into the modern age, specifically by fully computerizing the organization not only for completing mundane tasks but to fine-tune the direct marketing process. "Direct marketing is a very technical and mathematical discipline," he once said. By 1970, the managing of Jackson & Perkins fell into place, and Harry & David relocated its administrative offices, which had previously been near Los Angeles, back to Medford. These two events, according to John Holmes, "marked the second half of Bear Creek's modern era."

"The state of the art arrived pretty fast," says John Roberts, retired senior vice president of fruit acquisition. "John Holmes understood the need for it to manage the business." The computer quickly became a crucial component for maintaining superlative customer service, giving the company the capability to track thousands of orders, attend quickly to the rare customer complaint, update the ever-increasing mailing list, and analyze customer responses.

By the late 1960s, several million customers looked forward to receiving Harry & David's Christmas Book of Gifts. Harking back to the company's early beginnings when the high rollers of New York City jump-started the business with orders, the company formed a department exclusively devoted to the business-to-business channel, offering companies the opportunity to present customized incentive gifts to employees, suppliers, and customers.

▲ Shorter trees provide excellent fruit and high yield.

A Shorter (and Safer) Harvest

"The old ladders were just sixteen- to twenty-foot poles with steps on either side. Up at the very tip-top trying to reach the last pear, I've fallen off and come down through the trees looking like I'd been in a fight with a bobcat," says Marshall Sellers, talking of his many years in the orchard business." As a youngster, Sellers enjoyed being let out of school to "fill smudge" in the orchards, the sometimes dangerous practice of maintaining smudge pot operations to keep the trees from freezing during cold snaps. He and other young boys slept intermittently on cots and then awoke to run through the orchards, continually igniting the pots with lighted fluid. "We didn't have a lot of eyebrows in those days," he laughs. Sellers's first job at Harry & David was dumping peaches on a size-sorting belt. He climbed the not-so-dangerous corporate ladder until his retirement forty-seven years later as the director of fruit processing.

Shortly after Sellers joined Harry & David, Glenn Harrison traveled to France to study the dwarf pears grown there that produced three times the fruit as regular pear trees. Soon Bear Creek Orchards had grafted their Comice trees to quince root, which stunted the height of the usually twenty-five-foot trees. The first forty acres of the shorter and safer-to-harvest trees produced six tons per acre.

"Today pickers only need a three-tiered step to reach the pears, which is much easier and a lot safer," says Sellers. Though the days of running smudge are a fun memory, warming the orchards is now accomplished through eco-friendly windmills and clean-burning propane.

▲ **In the 1930s, gifts** by mail were only associated with Sears and Roebuck and a few seed companies. As this mail-order entry room shows, Harry & David soon changed that reality, first offering their pears as "Christmas gifts by mail."

The quaint jargon and communications in marketing materials may have depicted Harry & David as a mom-and-pop business, but it was now dealing with the demands and complications of a diverse corporation. "We own the dirt that the roots of our trees go into and the trees and fruit that grow from it," explains Bob Bluth, senior vice president and general counsel for the company today. "That means we deal with real estate, land use, agricultural issues, transportation, engineering, and every application from manufacturing to marketing. It's a very complex business."

David and John Holmes dealt with those complexities by tactically applying their complementary talents, and though they possessed differing personalities, both men contributed greatly to the continued success of the company.

"David could strike fear into the hearts of new people, but he was really a nice guy once you got to know him," says Roberts, also verifying a coworker's comment that David possessed a very dry wit. "John was a fun-loving guy. If he knew that someone was coming to visit him, his favorite trick was to get in his gorilla suit and come out of his office to meet them."

Dale Gooding worked for many years with Roberts and along with Roberts ascended the corporate ladder. In his thirty-four years with Harry & David, he rose from a cost accounting manager to executive vice president and chief operations officer. "One of the company's mainstays was promoting from within because of the particular expertise involved in such an operation," he says. Gooding remembers that he and his son played basketball with John Holmes and his son Jack. "At meetings John would put on the gorilla suit or the Cubby Bear outfit and be the life of the party for a while," he relates.

▲ **First hired to install a new cost accounting system** usable for Jackson & Perkins, and Harry & David, Dale Gooding wore many hats before retiring as executive vice president and chief operations officer. "Little did we know we'd stay here the rest of our lives," Gooding says of himself, John Roberts, and other coworkers who became close friends.

After handing the role of president over to his cousin John, David retained an office in Medford for a few years but spent more and more time on Arrowhead Ranch (a business he founded and operated), exercising his passion for raising horses and cattle. However, he acted as the chairman of the board for Harry & David and maintained an ongoing interest in the company for a number of years. "Even though David was living on his ranch, he would always write me a nice note regarding any promotion I received when it was announced in the paper," said Gooding. "He was one who always saw everyone at Harry & David as family."

A Cause for Roses

Harry & David sold the Jackson & Perkins Company in 2007, but during the forty years that Harry & David owned the business, the company made historical inroads with a product line of "Cause Roses." Although he would modestly say otherwise, the "Cause Rose" was the brainchild of Bill Ihle, executive vice president of corporate relations. "I met with the royal family to obtain the rights to use the name of Diana Princess of Wales for our rose," explains Ihle. "We gave 10 percent of the proceeds to the Diana Princess of Wales Memorial Fund, which goes primarily to land mine eradication and to purchase prostheses for land mine victims. We linked our name with one that had emotional connection with our customers, and also, along the way, we were able to do some good."

The approach continued to benefit other significant causes with the creation of the Veterans' Honor® Rose, which donates funds to veterans affected with diseases such as Agent Orange syndrome. (All of the roses in the White House Rose Garden were donated by none other than Jackson & Perkins, and Ihle even negotiated with the Vatican for the worldwide rights to name the Pope John Paul II rose.)

..no one does it better than Harry and David. **DETROIT NEWS**

Harry and David, an American tradition. **Sacramento BEE**

Harry and David best overall. A winning combination…. **Wall Street Journal**

…mouth water delights from Harry and David. **Miami Herald**

..everyone loves Harry and David **NBC Today Show**

Harry and David tour guides circa 1970

▲ **Of the company tour guides (circa 1970)** in this photo, Kay Armstrong (*far left*) is one of only two tour guides to date, approaching twenty years with Harry & David.

He did have a lighter side, but when it came to the company, John attended to every detail of business. Janiece Newell, who retired as the manager of legal services after forty years, recalls that John perused every word supplied by the then small marketing department. A two-fingered typist, he diligently revised and added comments until every message resonated with the friendly tone he wished to share with customers.

He did have a lighter side, but when it came to the company, John attended to every detail of business.

The Talented Son of a Founder

David H. Holmes, son of David H. Holmes Sr., died at the age of seventy-nine on August 19, 2002. After retiring as president of Harry & David in 1970, he founded Arrowhead Ranch in Medford and was its president and CEO. His employees may not have known that David was a bomber pilot in World War II and that he later founded Rogue Flying Service in Medford. In fact, among other aircraft, he owned a DC-3. He was also the captain and engineer of his own eighty-five-foot motor sailer (christened *Nereus*), an avid hunter, and a trainer and breeder of champion black Labrador retrievers and champion cutting horses. He and his wife, Brook, were married for twenty-six years, and he was the proud father of a daughter and three sons. After a full life, he passed away peacefully, surrounded by family and friends.

▲ **Harry & David employees share a common company** value: "Treat the customer the way you want to be treated. In short, you need to be a stickler for perfection, every step of the way."

In 1972, Bear Creek Corporation was formed as an umbrella for the multifaceted operations of Harry & David, including gift fruit, roses, imported gifts, and other businesses. In 1976, John took the company public, and by the early 1980s began considering offers for the still highly successful company that his father and uncle, so many years before, grew from the ground up. In 1984, he accepted an offer of $74.1 million from R. J. Reynolds Development Corp. of Winston-Salem, North Carolina. "Harry & David became a more sophisticated company under John, with more sophisticated marketing and production," stated longtime employee Perry Sneed. "John may have given the impression of being a reluctant president, but I think he loved it. We underwent exponential change during those years."

Agreeing to assist with the transition, upon his departure John Holmes personally gave every one of the company's one thousand employees a check for one thousand dollars to show his appreciation of their hard work and commitment to quality service. John's announcement of resignation to his loyal employees read in part:

> We have, individually and together, built a remarkable company in Bear Creek over the years, and it has been my privilege to be associated with you in this endeavor. As to the future, I believe it holds much promise.

John Holmes, ever a man of foresight, was absolutely right once again.

Booming Business
Brings Bigger Challenges

Though optical sorters add another level to quality inspection, the refined and specialized skill of the seasoned fruit sorter is very difficult to duplicate.

CHAPTER 5

BOOMING BUSINESS
BRINGS BIGGER CHALLENGES

After operating for years as an independent company and one of the largest of Oregon's businesses, Bear Creek Corporation now found itself owned by a somewhat indifferent parent. R. J. Reynolds, a multibillion-dollar organization, made its name in the tobacco industry, a vastly divergent pursuit from that of Harry & David. Just as the new management stepped in to make the changes that such buyouts often include, R. J. Reynolds participated in the biggest corporate merger of that time—the purchase of Nabisco Brands for $4.9 billion. Within a year, R. J. Reynolds had its financial hands full with merger issues. In 1986, Shaklee Corporation, a manufacturer and distributor of vitamins, minerals, and household products, purchased Bear Creek Corporation. Three years later, Yamanouchi Pharmaceutical Co. Ltd. of Tokyo, Japan, purchased both Shaklee and Bear Creek Corporation. Then touted by *Fortune* magazine as a "Global 500" best-performing company, Yamanouchi ushered Harry & David into the 1990s, a decade of incredible growth and innovation.

In 1988, a newly hired president and CEO, Bill Williams, immediately began gathering an executive team with expertise in retail, direct marketing, logistics, and information technology. "We had a lot on our plate in the 1990s including increasing catalog circulation, launching the Harry & David retail stores, improving computer information systems, adding new orchards,

With pears, everything comes off the tree quickly, because frost can be a very limiting and expensive factor.

the advent of Internet sales, and improving the physical infrastructure of the production and administrative facilities," he remembers.

Don Cato, senior vice president and general manager of customer operations, joined the company with many years of experience in the department store industry, marketing, merchandising, and operations. "The retail stores were an avenue for excess production capacity and a way to get more countercyclical sales into the organization," Cato explains. "While those efforts have come to fruition and although we have about 140 stores out there today, the nature of that peak season still remains. Those stores still have a significant spike during the holiday season."

▼ **The cooler wall at Harry & David's Country**
Village store is a great place to find the most desirable foods and beverages for chilling out.

◀ **In the "Big Red" facility, highly skilled**
sorters select and pack premium pears.

▲ **Kay Guches boxes a bunch of Moose Munch® Confection.**
Like many of her fellow employees and often their families,
Guches has enjoyed a long career—thirty-four years with
Harry & David.

Cato's team manages any operations related to customer support, which means oversight of the call centers and the distribution centers spread strategically around the country. "We ship gifts to the distribution centers, and they in turn ship to the recipients, so we can make timely deliveries when the holiday season is upon us," Cato says. A $34 million facility in Hebron, Ohio—the Hopewell Center (a distribution, call center, and assembly operation) added in 1997—complements the central call center in Medford and a seasonal call center in Eugene, Oregon, providing customers with around-the-clock, coast-to-coast service.

Because of the difficulty of shipping perishables internationally, Harry & David focuses on national sales but boasts of a growing Canadian market. "Because of the international agricultural laws, many countries stop product at the port of entry for inspection, in some

▲ **Carolyn McAlmond shows that careful**
sorting and packing continues to be a
hands-on tradition.

cases for an entire day, which is just a nemesis to a pear," Cato says, explaining the company's decision to limit international trade.

With the business channels of direct marketing (including Internet and catalogs), the stores division, wholesale (with retailers such as Costco, Target, and Macy's), and business-to-business markets, this vertically integrated company demands flexibility of its staff and employees. "There are times when I have wholesale product, retail stores product, and a transfer to one of the distribution centers all on the same truck," says Cato.

▲ **Bill Ihle, executive vice president corporate relations; Nancy Reagan, former first lady;** Nancy Tait, former president; and Leigh Johnson, vice president government relations, gather around a dozen debut honorees of the Jackson & Perkins Nancy Reagan rose.

The Traveling Pear

Even with such a perishable product as the pear, shipping is a cinch compared to the years before refrigerated trucking and freight cars existed. "Pears ripen during the transition, so they were extremely careful," says Don Cato, senior vice president and general manager of customer operations, referring to former times. "But obviously when they reached the recipient, those pears were ready to eat. No doubt about it, they did a lot of magical things back then."

▲ **Marshall Sellers, retired director of** fruit processing.

Magical indeed. Marshall Sellers, retired director of fruit processing, remembers when the gifts were once packed in boxcars that were either diesel-engine cooled or iced and shipped to sidings "for a month or two prior to Christmas," he says. "We tried to get the gifts into the closest zones so that the postage was less. The post office actually came to the rail station as we pulled the gifts out of the railcars, attached the labels and postage, and put it in their trucks. Then they delivered it locally."

Today, the pears are predominantly shipped by refrigerated truck with painstaking rules for quality preservation. "We are very picky about the temperature because the fruit will overripen if not kept within a very narrow temperature range," explains Pete Kratz, executive vice president of operations and wholesale. "The trailers are set to maintain that temperature." In addition, the delicate pears require storage in a refrigerated space of exacting air flow, humidity, and venting standards. "Here everything has its own storage and shipping requirements, meaning that we put a lot of fruit and product together in a gift that can't be stored together, so when we assemble it, we expedite shipment to the customer. We pack on demand," says Kratz.

"The Internet made a dramatic impact on the business because it changed the technology of how people ordered. When the store concept was rolled out, that was a major change from going from a catalog company to a multi-channel business," comments Joe Foley, senior vice president and general manager, stores division.

Harry & David's original Web site, launched in 1996, was at first viewed as a communications piece with a few product offerings. However, as online commerce expanded, so did Harry & David's Internet business. Internet sales account for as much as 60 percent of direct marketing orders today, so much so that a special call center customer service team supports any Web questions, answering customer queries within twenty-four hours or less. "The growth of the Internet channel has been steady. Our call centers would take ninety thousand calls on our peak days. The Internet has kept that volume from growing," agrees Tom Forsythe, senior vice president of production.

▲ **Joe Foley, senior vice** president and general manager, stores division.

◄ **A good picker picks one bin or better per hour,** according to Ron Henri, retired senior vice president of orchards.

▲ **Robbie Merriman, with twenty-eight years of** service with the company, sorts and packs peaches. A bruised peach will not get past these pros.

Pete Kratz, executive vice president of operations and wholesale, admits that when the Internet business came on like gangbusters, it served up a pleasant surprise. "If we didn't have Internet sales, we would have to have more call centers across the U.S.," he explains. "Otherwise we would have to double the size of our call centers. It came at a great time and allowed us to use the assets that we have efficiently."

Mother's Day, Valentine's Day, Halloween, and Thanksgiving: Harry & David catalogs weren't just for Christmas anymore. During the 1990s, these special holiday planner catalogs were added to the original issue, which had more than doubled in size. Expanding business meant expanding demands for infrastructure. In addition to the Hopewell Center, the organization built an Education & Employment Center and Information Technology Building, and added extensively both to the packinghouse and the Candy Kitchen & Bakery. Meanwhile, the company planted more orchards and improved its cold storage facilities.

"During the 1990s, we experienced the biggest sales and profit growth in the company's history," states Bill Williams, president and CEO. "We more than doubled in size in every aspect, and it was a period of great renovation, modernization, and expansion." Predicting at the time that the success of these strategic initiatives would carry into the next decade, Williams, like his predecessor John Holmes, was right on target.

Wind, Hail, and Fire

Since the company's first fruit trees took root in the rich soil of the Rogue River Valley, the founders, heirs, and employees of Harry & David have learned to rebound from an endless array of challenges, most dealt unpredictably by Mother Nature's hand. In 1962, winds destroyed half a million dollars worth of Comice pears. In the early 1980s, again high winds destroyed almost 60 percent of the Comice crop, prompting the company to mitigate such future risks by spreading plantings in numerous places across the valley floor and planting towering poplar trees nearby for wind blockage.

Nancy Tait, retired president of Bear Creek Corporation, remembers facing a weather-related crisis following a tumultuous thunderstorm with hail. She distinctly recalls the morning after that storm, which was also her first day on the job with Harry & David over two decades ago: "I walk in the door and within five minutes an emergency meeting was called. 'Five percent of the crop is on the ground and we've got to strategize what we are going to do!' I hadn't considered the fact that a thunderstorm could be so hurtful to the business. I remember that first day thinking, *Oh my gosh, what have I gotten myself into?*"

A dramatic fall in the stock market in the late 1980s certainly didn't help the large business-to-business gift market, but one of the most devastating disasters occurred in October 1996—a major fire in one of Harry & David's seasonal facilities. The distribution centers are but one aspect of Don Cato's many responsibilities. After receiving news of the blaze in the middle of the night, he attended a predawn meeting and immediately boarded a plane to the location. "It was still burning when I got there," he recalls. "It was just devastating, really quite an ordeal for the company, and one of the most catastrophic events we've faced." Just prior to peak season, the company had lost a lot of perishable product in addition to vast losses in other products. "Within two and a half weeks we had located an alternative facility and were up and shipping. It sure made for an interesting peak season, but we managed to get ourselves back on track, and customers were well served," Cato concludes.

The Old West philosophy of dusting oneself off and starting over again appears to run through the veins of the Harry & David staff. For them, barriers become challenges and challenges become victories. Bob Bluth, general counsel, seems to speak not only for himself but all of his colleagues when he states, "One of the incredibly fascinating things about this company to me is the huge spectrum of what goes on. I have yet to be able to predict at the beginning of any day what will happen, and that's a good thing."

▲ **Don Cato, senior vice president and** general manager of customer operations.

▲ **Bob Bluth, senior vice president and general** counsel, says of his work at Harry & David, "My life is one of continual learning. I love what I do here."

A Care-Full Culture

Visitors from around the country begin and end their tour of the company by browsing the aisles and buying scrumptious souvenirs from Harry & David's Country Village flagship store.

CHAPTER 6

A CARE-FULL CULTURE

Mouthwatering raspberry cheesecakes rest on racks near large convection ovens. Upon cooling, they'll enter a blast freezer that prepares them for packaging. A skilled associate precisely arranges groups of several small dough dots on a conveyor belt—dots that will soon bake into delicious cookies. Employees standing near bowls of swirling chocolate look up at the tour groups peering down from elevated walkways; both groups wave and smile. The company staff seem to be enjoying themselves as much as the onlookers who at any given time may come from another state, another country, or just a local school or business to observe how Harry & David creates the delectable products that are famous worldwide.

The sixty-thousand-square-foot bakery/candy kitchen produces baklava, cookies, layer cake, chocolate-covered fruits, smores graham crackers, sixteen flavors of Moose Munch® caramel-coated popcorn mix, truffles with delicious flavored centers, and more, more, more. The chocolate, oh the chocolate! It's the Harry & David special blend. Automated vertical form-fill machines rapidly deposit sesame stick crackers and other pleasing snacks into decorative bags, while stomachs growl and taste buds tingle just from breathing the air. Some of these items—along with the pears, peaches, and a variety of delicious fruits—will soon be joined in a beautiful basket packed with care by employees trained to assemble each gift as though it would be sent to their own mothers, grandmothers, and other special friends and relatives. And each and every item, each final package is perfection.

Only the best of berries, such as these dark, sweet cherries, are selected by Harry & David.

With approximately sixty thousand square feet of bakery and candy kitchens, goodies galore fill the air with mouthwatering aromas.

Sun-ripe Strawberry; Red, White & Blueberry; Peach Mango; German Chocolate; Banana Caramel . . . Are you ready for some of Harry & David's supremely delicious cheesecake?

When Harry & David gifts arrive at customers' doors, those grateful recipients can hardly imagine the intricate industry of detail behind each product. Internally, the folks at Harry & David think of it as a complete process—"from the farm to the customer's door"—as they nurture their product every step of the way until they release each artistic assemblage to its lucky recipient. At one time, Harry & David produced signature canned fruits, preserves, sauces, relishes, and vinegars, but those endeavors eventually were contracted to quality suppliers or were dropped from the product line. Yet approximately 80 percent of all Harry & David products continue to be packaged onsite. "Of the eighteen thousand tons of peaches and pears that we'll harvest this year, only 50 percent of it will make our gift standard," explains Tom Forsythe, senior vice president of production. The remaining fruit will go to

Connie Dalton tempts the world with another creation from the research kitchen.

Kay Armstrong, a Harry & David tour guide for two decades, points out the route for a group touring the facility.

Chocolate for a Lifetime

"The idea kitchen offers a world of experimentation for Harry & David's onsite food scientists. "You can come to our scientists and ask for a yellow brownie that tastes like cherries, and with not much more information than that, they'll formulate it, produce samples, and scale it up to thousands of pounds," says Tom Forsythe. "A lot of talent occupies this space."

One of those talents is Charlie Douglass, whose official title is manager, research and development of confection and food processing; he is more commonly known as the chocolatier. A third-generation candy maker, Douglass began apprenticing at age nine with an elderly Swiss candy maker

▲ **In a Money magazine multibrand taste test,** Harry & David's Grand Collection bested top-of-the-market brands such as Godiva. "It's not just the chocolate itself," says Charlie Douglass, chocolatier. "It's the high-quality tastes we put together and the taste profiles we offer."

at his family's confectionary in New Jersey. Like many Harry & David associates, he's held many positions in his twenty-nine years with the company, but has settled happily into his expertise developing the chocolate candies that have made the company's special blend famous in the industry.

Surprisingly, the responsibilities of a chocolatier are numerous, from proportioning recipes for mass production, to retrofitting equipment, to constantly inventing new products for the talented merchants of the stores, wholesale, and catalog divisions that select products for upcoming seasons. "Usually a concept is there, but when you're actually creating, there is a lot of leeway to play with serendipitous ideas. That's where interesting things happen," says Douglass.

Talking to Charlie the chocolatier invites visions of sugarplums and truffles as he discusses praline centers, burnt sugar caramel fillings, and the "one-shot" machine that creates a chocolate shell and fills it simultaneously with a rich "flowy" center. Currently Harry & David uses approximately 7 million pounds of chocolate a year, but Douglass never tires of the sweet. Charlie relates that when people discover that he creates chocolate candies for Harry & David, they often exclaim, "Man, you've got a dream job!"

"And I can't help but answer, 'You know what? I think I do!'" he says.

supermarkets or will be processed into purees. Large bins of pears are simply not gift quality, but are still suitable as produce. Some of them will be given away to charitable groups throughout the region, reflecting the community service core of Harry & David's waste-not, want-not values.

Beeps, blaring horns, the deafening roar of engines, and vehicles on the move blast the silence of the serene mountainous backdrop of Harry & David's headquarters. Here, "from farm to door" is a theme set in perpetual motion. The roads of the company's Forklift Pathway are without speed bumps and are limited to "forklift traffic only" as a precaution against any impacts that might bruise the precious fruit. "Eggs are actually more resilient than our pears," explains Forsythe. The summertime scent of peaches, trucked ripe from the fields, wafts through the air as they are placed immediately in cool storage prior to the sorting process, a process that for years was completed first by size-belt sorts and then solely by hand under the trained eyes of skilled selectors.

Today, Harry & David's state-of-the art optical sorter rolls the fruit through an ice-cold river of water where each piece is scanned and sorted in groups for color contrast and size. Next the sorter determines (with infrared light) the sweetest pears based on brix (or sugar content). "Peaches may bruise easier, but a bruise to a pear will have longer-lasting impact. A bruise spot on a peach won't

◀ **"Pack on demand is when you marry up products that require** two different temperatures and expedite shipment," says Tom Forsythe, senior vice president of production, explaining the activity that takes place here in the "5th Barrel" building.

At Harry & David's Country Village store, customers' baskets runneth over with fresh offerings from the field. The company also regularly donates fruit to local charities.

Moose Munch®: You Can't Stop Eating It!

Possibly not since the Fruit-of-the-Month Club® gift has a Harry & David product packed a punch like Moose Munch® Confection. The popularity of the popcorn-based confection (originally in toffee flavor) exploded so quickly that fans can now devour the buttery, nutty, spicy,

or sweet crunchy treat in an expanding number of flavors. Moose Munch® Confection is a caramel-coated popcorn that may also be enrobed/coated in chocolate and paired with an irresistible and infinite number of edibles.

Caramel, milk chocolate, dark chocolate, cranberry-almond, caramel-apple, butter pecan, barbecue cheddar cheese, jalapeño, ranch, and an assortment of seasonal flavors fly off the shelves so fast that Harry & David has had to hastily adjust its production capabilities.

"We've struggled to keep up with the yearly rise in demand for Moose Munch® Confection," says Pete Kratz, executive vice president of operations and wholesale. "We put in a new line and then a year later had to double the capacity."

Once developed—after sampling approximately 165 taste profiles—from the finest chocolate, whole nuts, caramels, and other ingredients, Harry & David needed only a name reminiscent of the product's northwestern origins. Stores merchant Paula Rogers-Brandt suggested the snacky and whimsical ® name, a name that stuck, along with the memory of its unforgettable tastiness. Today, the product line is continually growing to include plush toys, candy bars, fudge, and even new blends of aromatic coffee. Currently Harry & David produces approximately 5 million pounds of Moose Munch® Confection per year. "Moose Munch® Confection is almost addictive," says Cathy Fultineer, executive vice president of brand management and product innovation. "People are fanatical about it, and we think it's the best."

▲ **Filling bags with Moose Munch® Confection** may become tempting for those working in Harry & David's bakery/candy kitchen, but the customer always comes first!

Pete Kratz, executive vice president ▶ of operations and wholesale.

Travelers pull off of the interstate to visit Harry & David's Country Village store in Medford, Oregon, and few, if any of them, leave with empty hands.

get past the packers, but the slight rubbing of a pear isn't immediately visible and it might turn black later. I don't know of anyone else in the United States using this type of technology for pears," states Forsythe. Still, more inspection by skilled human sorters is required before they wrap any piece of gift fruit in the signature tissue paper of Harry & David.

The fruit, a component with demands that can't be ignored, must be married in varying temperatures with numerous products with equally specific requirements for care. Some baskets are completed by an assembly process in which packagers add one or two components into each basket as it passes by. Many other baskets are completed in a kitting process in which one person packs an entire basket. In either case, packagers have the discretion, indeed the responsibility, to reject any product that is flawed even in the slightest way.

Before any of this can occur, repetitive prototypes of each gift basket have been constructed and tested on equipment that shakes, rattles, rolls—and even drops—the product to ensure that all will transport intact. "You can always design something that looks wonderful, but if you can't

◀ *(From left)* **Past employee** Suzanne Morse, and Rhonda Klug of corporate relations, with twenty-two years of service, join Cheryl Smith, a Country Village basket maker, and her associate in showing off a bountiful Harry & David gift.

ship it, you have to go back and redesign or substitute a different product," explains Perry Higgins, vice president of quality control.

For years the company hand-tied every bow that was attached to the gift packages, each distinctive ribbon passing under the watchful eye of Glenn Harrison, the company's quality overseer. "We used to have an army of women that tied bows all summer long. We topped out at about 650,000 bows per season," states Higgins. One employee tied bows for the company into her nineties. Much of that operation is now automated, but Harry & David still hand-ties approximately 150,000 specialty bows per season for custom gifts.

This quality emphasis is part and parcel of employee training and the exacting standards asked of every associate. Employees regularly participate in voluntary panels in which they enter sensory booths to test products and fruit for appearance, flavor, texture, and overall acceptance. Such practices exemplify the way Harry & David shows all associates that they indeed play an integral role in the company's success.

Over the years the company has received abundant correspondence thanking these basket assemblers personally.

When a personally produced basket is complete, the assembler adds a note card containing his or her signature. Over the years the company has received abundant correspondence thanking these basket assemblers personally. "We want our employees to understand that we are not a food company," says Higgins. "You need to pack that box of pears like you would deliver it to your family member or friend, because it's going to have your name on it. First and foremost, we are building a gift."

A Quality Future

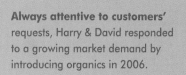

CHAPTER 7

A QUALITY FUTURE

Today the towered, art-deco building that housed Harry & David's first production plant proudly faces the South Pacific Highway, though now it is surrounded by the modern headquarters, office buildings, and numerous round-topped cold storage, warehouse, and assembly areas called "barrels" by Harry & David insiders. One of the first buildings of this vast complex, the only original remaining pieces of the structure, are its towers and wooden framework. The rest of the building underwent a $2.5 million conversion in 1985, but today the Old Packinghouse is getting another facelift. "You can see that the old sign has been taken down. One of my projects is to replace the sign with the newest Harry & David script instead of the blocky letters that were there before," says Ed Snyder, project engineer. Snyder and fellow engineer Dick Richardson have taken part in managing the continually changing landscape of the operations for decades. During Snyder's twenty-nine years with the company, the sprawling complex has necessarily experienced growth spurts to meet, and anticipate, production and technological demands.

"There's always modernization going on, production efficiency, and projects to automate more and more," he explains. "We're always aware that we have to maintain the highest quality possible for the product, so a lot of our projects are geared toward maintaining the quality."

This optical fruit sorter is just one example of Harry & David's use of current technologies. It scans and sorts fruit, providing efficiency while making quality even more consistent.

▲ **Describing the 1990s as a period of "great renovation, modernization, and expansion,"** Bill Williams, president and CEO, noted that the company almost tripled in size in every aspect during that time. A major addition included an expanded headquarters building, its South Lobby entrance pictured here.

Quality: it's a word used often by Harry & David associates and staff, but here it is not merely a bandied-about buzzword; it is a core-value mantra. Following the sale of Harry & David in 2004, majority owned by Wasserstein & Co, LP, has only redoubled that commitment. After that purchase, president and CEO Bill Williams, in a letter to his employees, stated, "Recent investments in infrastructure such as orchards, facilities, equipment, and IT systems place us in a favorable position to control operating costs. . . . Under new ownership, we begin an important and exciting new period of our history. Our customers can look forward to the great quality and service they have come to expect from Harry & David."

"Our customers can look forward to the great quality and service they have come to expect from Harry & David."

Exceeding expectations means continual evolution in terms of environmental concerns, employee and public relations, and product offerings: Harry & David sprints ahead in all of those terrains. "We like to say that Harry & David was green before green was cool," says Rudd Johnson, executive vice president of human resources. "Many years ago before people were talking about organic, we chose to systematically limit our use of spray applications and were looking into conceivable ways to use methods that were more earth friendly. And today we have certified organic orchards." Harry & David projected ninety-four acres of organic orchards in 2009, yielding seven hundred tons of pears. Johnson notes that when he joined the company, major recycling initiatives for paper, aluminum, and plastics; a focus to find practical and feasible recyclable products; and clean water storm drain projects were already entrenched, long before environmental issues were a national focus. "It's a robust program that has been going on for a long time, not just to save money but because it's the right thing to do," says Johnson.

▲ **Rudd Johnson, executive vice president of** human resources.

◄ **Retired president Nancy Tait (*right*)** showing then mayor Lindsay Berryman the company's recycling program. Harry & David won the U.S. Conference of Mayors Recycling at Work Award in 2001.

▲ **Paul Todak, with twenty-three years of service, is produce manager** of the Harry & David Country Village, where Harry & David retirees enjoy a lifetime discount.

Organic crops have become a bigger part of production each year. Harry & David's commitment to sustainable agriculture also pleases the community.

Ahead of the game already with a program for sustainability, this company sees it as part of an overall strategy for current and future management. "Sustainability is not only about recycling, pollution abatement, and energy conservation," states Pete Kratz, who also serves as a member of the Sustainability Board of Oregon. "It involves using responsible methods in everything we do, including treating employees right and supporting the community."

"I remember the people the most," says Dale Gooding, who retired after thirty-four years with the company. "We not only have high-quality service and products, but high-quality people." Goodwill and reciprocity sustain an involved, productive, and growth-oriented workforce, which is why an open-door policy for all employees is not just a slogan at Harry & David. Associates don't have to wade through a strict chain of command to find answers to questions or resolutions to problems. "Anybody can call me and make an appointment to see me," says Rudd Johnson. But associates' concerns seldom need to reach the executive level because the company doesn't sequester its human resources personnel away in a single office. Rather, Harry & David embeds them within the workforce—the bakery/candy kitchen, the call center, the distribution centers—where the HR associates are readily accessible to help resolve any problems.

Harry & David associates and executives remain inextricably involved with giving back to the community that has made its success possible. In addition to a myriad of outreach programs, the company proudly acts as the single largest contributor to United Way in its home county of Jackson. In fact, a late employee, Teresa McCormick, had the idea to partner with United Way by opening a year-round agency on campus to help both full-time and seasonal

▲ Shown here *(far left)* is John Daily, retired chief financial officer. Harry & David is the single largest contributor to the United Way in Jackson County, and the company provides a United Way facility on campus for employees and their families.

The Perfect Order

Surrounded by coworkers in Harry & David's vast Medford, Oregon, call center, Georgene Richardson, call center associate, remains focused on her customers. One caller has a question about how pears ripen, another about the consistency of a cheese product, another wants to send a Harry & David gift with a thank-you note enclosed. Richardson listens patiently and responds warmly to each person. During a brief lull, she takes a breath and explains that call center workers add customer notes to gifts for occasions such as birthdays, anniversaries, even personal loss. "The sympathy notes are the hardest," she says, demonstrating the individual care that these call center associates give to every client.

The care is reciprocated by an employer who keeps call center staff happy with regular recognition, fun contests, and incentives that make their work varied and challenging. A number of bulletin boards display letters and notes from pleased customers. "We get lots of nice words from customers complimenting our products and services," says Kristen Winter, former vice president of the call center. "We try to capture and post those that include an associate's name."

Such efforts result in an unusually high retention rate for a call center with an average employment tenure of nine years. Harry & David employs year-round core staff in its two call centers— at peak season approximately thirty-seven hundred people—who field incoming calls, take orders, and answer questions. "During most

▲ Harry & David's customer operations and call center personnel handle approximately four thousand calls per day in the off season. That number jumps almost twenty times during the holidays.

of the year we handle thirty-five hundred to four thousand calls a day, but in the holiday season we're up over the seventy thousand range," says Winter. When these call center operators make follow-up calls or contact customers regarding new products, they receive warm welcomes. "Our customers don't hang up on us," says Winter. "They even call us back when they see we've called."

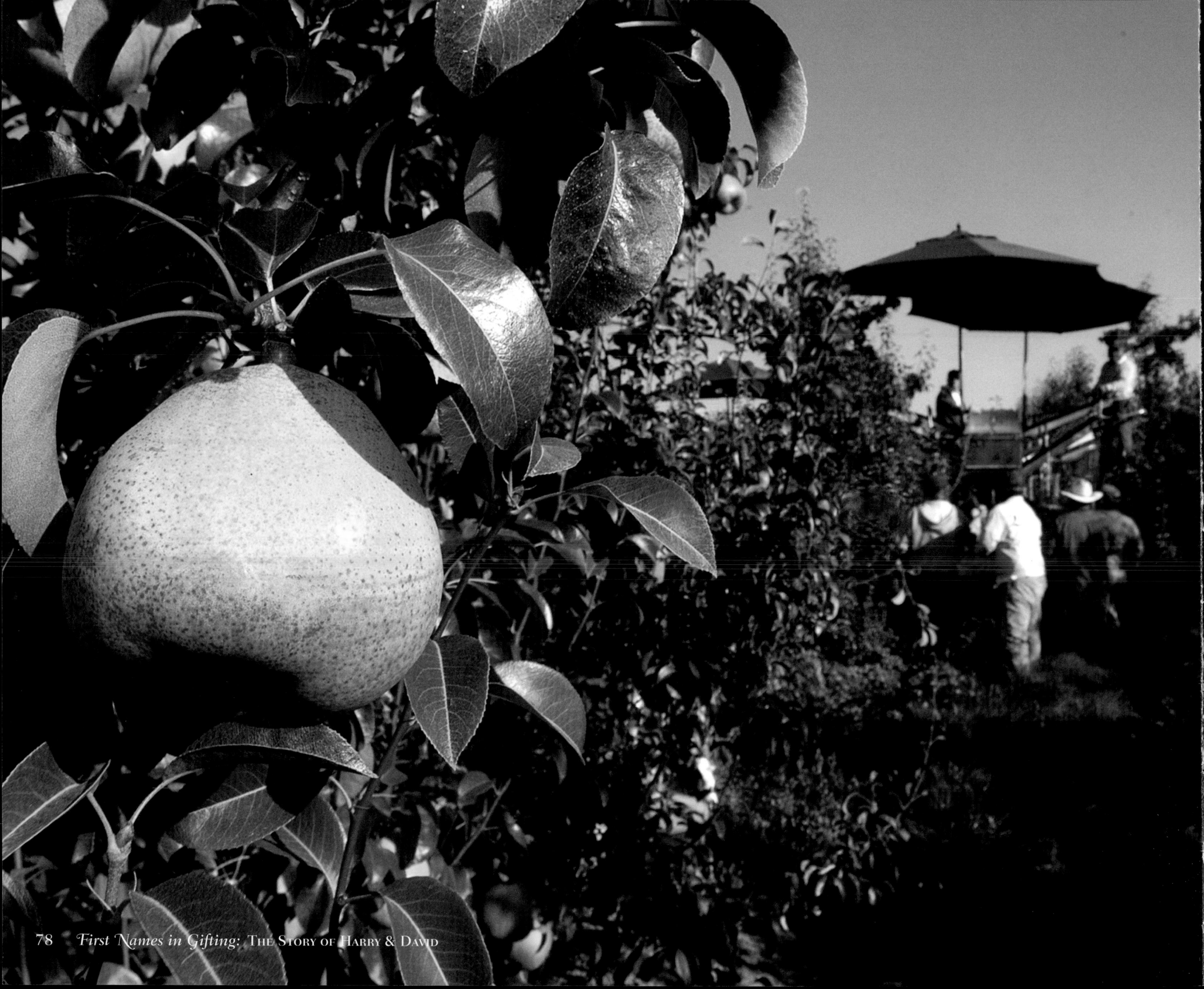

employees who were facing any significant personal or financial problems. The resulting employee assistance center—which helps employees deal with anything from a death in the family, to illness, to legal issues, to navigating complex community systems—is dedicated in her name.

This dedication not just to quality service and product but to quality employee relations results in a workforce that includes three and four generations of families and employees who remain with the company throughout their careers. Even when those careers are ended, those leaving after decades of service are treated to a gala celebration at the biggest ballroom in town, and, along with other earned retirement benefits, they receive a lifetime discount on the products they worked so proudly to produce. "We deliver quality products and we try to deliver a quality work experience to our

Some pickers live locally, and some return seasonally. Good rapport, available housing, and a wonderful meal service means that, typically, 92 percent of the workers return each year.

(Left)
Yes, there is a proper way to pick a pear, and individuals who know the trick harvest up to four hundred pounds per hour.

(Opposite page)
Currently, Bear Creek Orchards yields about eighteen thousand tons of Comice pears per year. Of that, less than 50 percent are Royal Riviera® quality.

"We deliver quality products and we try to deliver a quality work experience to our employees, and we have high standards," states Johnson.

Honoring the Troops

Bill Ihle, executive vice president of corporate relations, recently met with National Guard personnel to make sure that every one of Oregon's nine hundred soldiers based in Afghanistan received a holiday gift from Harry & David. A commander on leave later visited the company's headquarters to personally thank the employees of Harry & David, informing them that several of the gifts were even delivered on the backs of burros to soldiers in remote locations. Harry & David also received numerous thank-you notes, some written on paper towels or a scrap of cardboard, from many grateful soldiers. The effort represents the sincere outreach of an organization that truly lives its values. "It's not a political statement," says Ihle. "These soldiers are on the other side of the world, and they need to understand that someone at home is thinking of them and telling them that they are important."

▲ **Every year, Harry & David sends holiday gifts and cards** to Oregon's soldiers stationed around the world.

employees, and we have high standards," states Johnson.

Cathy Fultineer, executive vice president of brand management and product innovations, speaking of an emphasis to groom and promote employees from within the organization, puts it this way: "We grow pears; we might as well grow people."

"We have fruit, we have baked goods, we have confections, and they all go together to create the wonderful picture of the perfect gift. Our whole idea is to delight people. That's what we're here to do," says Charlie Douglass, chocolatier.

▲ **Cathy Fultineer, executive vice president** of brand management and product innovations states, "Our tradition of excellence is not only in the food quality, but in the design and presentation, and the quality of the customer experience."

And no one puts more emphasis on spreading knowledge of those products to the world than Bill Ihle, executive vice president of corporate relations. Traveling up to two hundred thousand miles annually, Ihle promotes the company's products like a man with a mission—a mission to reach a continually growing audience each year. Last year, via the *Today* show, *Good Morning*

◀ **No destination is too far and no venue** too difficult for Bill Ilhe, who travels up to two hundred thousand miles a year promoting the Harry & David brand. His meetings, visits, and media appearances are always positive publicity for the company's products, quality, and community citizenship.

America, Food Network appearances, countless local TV appearances, and print media, the company spoke to over a billion people. "We have an amazing product, and people want to talk with us," states Ihle.

Recently the product line expanded when Harry & David acquired Wolferman's, renowned for its premium English muffins and breakfast products, and Cushman's, a Florida-based fruit company famous for its Honeybells (a rare hybrid of tangerine and grapefruit). "The thing to remember about both of these brands is they have a very unique signature product of their own," explains Fultineer. "We have made sure to acquire companies that have that unique point of difference, because we believe that is very essential to being successful in the specialty food and gift market." That success has resulted in more than $500 million in annual sales.

An aerial view of the orchards during harvest reveals the infrastructure of roads that allows for gentle and prompt transport to the loading yards.

A Tradition of Leadership

"There's a man who works in the upper corner of this building who encourages people to excel. He has a sense of history and what a company ought to be," says Bob Bluth, senior vice president and general counsel.

"He is a bright non-egotistical, talented, I-get-it CEO, and a pleasure to work with," says Bill Ihle, executive vice president, corporate relations.

These are but a few of the accolades describing Bill Williams, president and chief executive officer of Harry & David since 1988. As the corporate leader for almost a third of Harry & David's existence, Williams has guided the company through continually changing business challenges, while ensuring one element remains steadfast: the culture's commitment to improvement. "At Harry & David, the people are hardworking, honest, and want to do the right thing by others," says Williams. "These aren't traits I insisted on when I came on board. The people of Harry & David have been this way since the beginning of this company, through generations of workers. It's an ethic that has been firmly ingrained here."

An employee open-door policy, personal attention to every customer, a 100 percent satisfaction guarantee, and employee community involvement—all exemplify the quality environment that Williams supports. Of course, a company that farms the land extends concern for the environment beyond the office walls. "We have agricultural roots and consider ourselves stewards of the environment, we apply those principles to all we do," states Williams.

Actively involved in both his company and community, Williams continues to take Harry & David toward its goal of becoming a billion-dollar enterprise. Ultimately, Williams attributes the stability of the company to a set of crucial company-wide values: "Gifting is a fluid business, and the effort required to continually fulfill our customers' wishes requires enormous planning. But this company has always risen to the occasion and learned from its mistakes. If we always keep the end goal in mind—a satisfied customer who feels they've been treated right, whether they're receiving a gift or giving one—then Harry & David will thrive for another seventy-five years."

Bill Williams, president and chief executive officer, cultivates a culture that treats employees and customers as valued family members. "Together we strive to satisfy our customers who entrust us to deliver their best wishes and gifts. This goal has remained the same throughout Harry & David's seventy-five-year history," he says.

As part of its expanding gift offerings, Harry & David gift recipients now can toast with a glass of fine wine from a gift basket. Fultineer sees expansion into new products as increasingly important, as will be any and all future acquisitions and partnerships. "Our marketing story is about the integrity of our product that comes from our tradition in excellence, not only in the quality of our product and presentation, but the quality of the customer service and experience. Since 1934, that's what we stand for," she says.

The culture at Harry & David is one of intense pride in product and tradition, with a drive to always look with open minds and hearts to the future, just as two brothers did so many years ago when the entire fate of the organization rested on a pear orchard. Somehow the seed that was planted then has rooted itself soundly in a diverse but close family tree. "Another generation will succeed us, and another will succeed them," concludes Ihle. "We're simply the caretakers of this brand that two brothers started seventy-five years ago . . . and that's such a privilege."

The dawn breaks on a frosty morning, greeting the first signs of spring. Green, finely toothed, oval leaves glisten in the sharp air as the sun makes its climb up the rugged mountain range to welcome and coax the future fruit of the Rogue River Valley to grow and prosper.

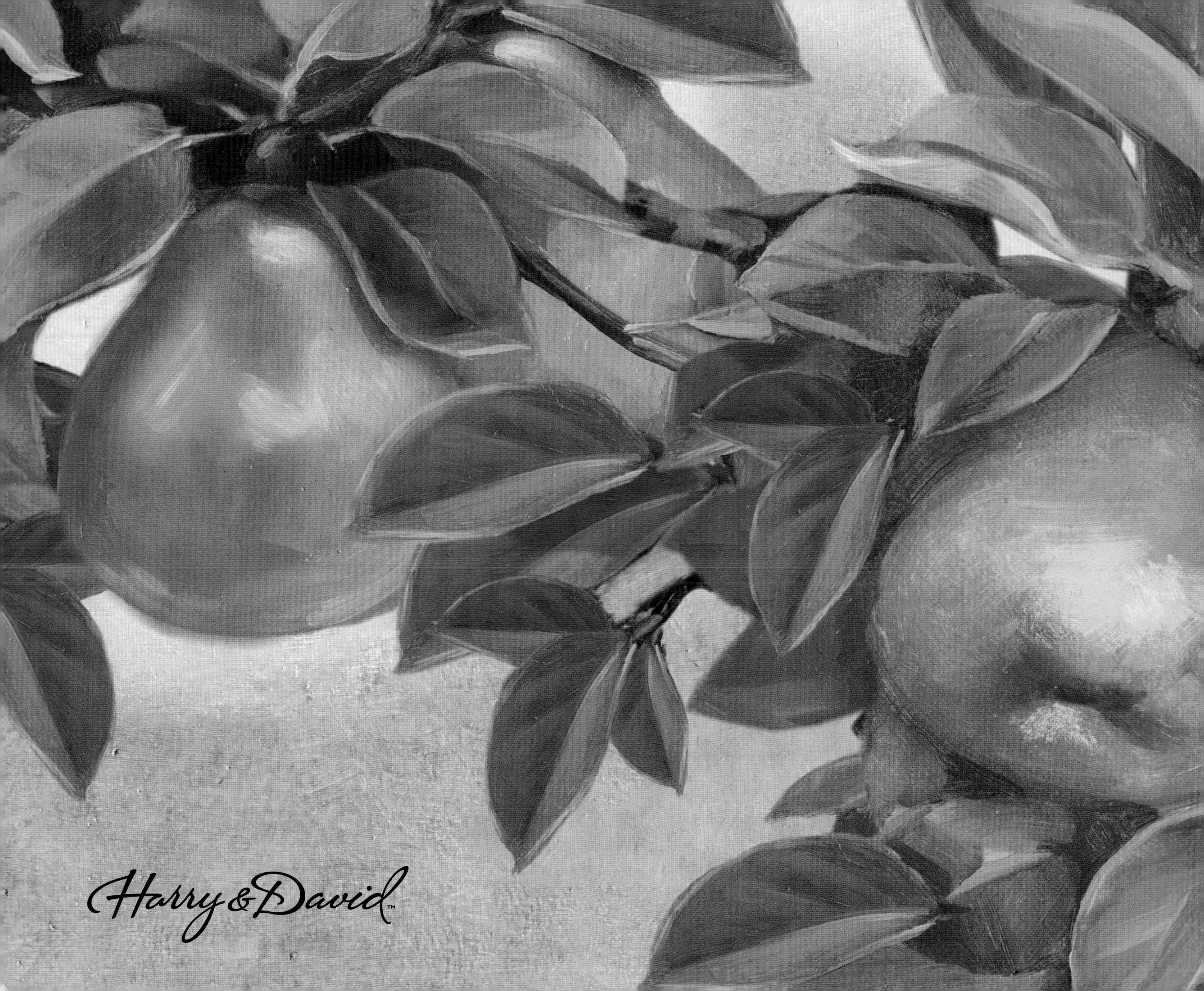
Harry & David™

INDEX